Journey Up The Gravel Path

Journey Up The Gravel Path
By Denise O'Brien-Peterson

ISBN 13: 978-1499547924

Cover and Interior Design by T.L. Price Freelance
Cover image by iStockphoto

Acknowledgments

2013 was a year of many highs and lows, and my experiences during the year made me pursue writing this book.

I am extremely grateful for the love, support, and care I was given by the following people:

My loving husband, Ron Peterson and my "happiness" Zachary Peterson – Without the two of you, I would not be the wife and mom I am today.

Mom and Dad – I will do my best to not scare the daylights out of you again. I love you, and look forward to watching you enjoy being grandparents to Zachary. Thank you for raising me to be a strong woman.

Keelie, Mackenzie, and Cameron – You are the strongest kids I have ever met, and your futures are extremely bright. You make me very proud!

Barbara – Thank you for everything; from babysitting to hospital visits, to cooking meals, prayers and thoughtful check in's. We really couldn't have done it without you. We love you!

Jen, Alison, Lisa, Leslie, Sandy, Marnie, Gina, and Julianne – Thank you for your hospital visits, taking care of Zachary and for keeping me in the right frame of mind. The laughs always come naturally with all of you in my life.

Robyn – Thank you for helping secure a second opinion, and for reassuring us, I was receiving the best medical treatment possible. Your willingness to talk to others in the medical field helped put our minds at ease, and we are forever grateful.

To all of my friends who sent messages, cards, food, flowers and visited or called. Thank you for your support. I am very lucky to call you my friends.

Dave and Diane – Thank you for the many hospital visits, for taking care of Zachary, and for being incredibly supportive.

Dr. Rabin – Thank you for keeping your nose in those medical books, being a terrific neurosurgeon, and removing my tumor. I am healthy and tumor free thanks to you.

Brenda – Thank you for helping me see there is a way to bring my story to others, and for introducing me to people who could teach me how to make my dream a reality.

Dr. Kwon – The day you gave me the okay to ride my bike again was one of the best days of my radiation treatments. Your approach to radiation was unlike anything I could have ever expected. Thank you for taking the best care of me and my family.

To my co-workers in Chicagoland and Virginia – Thank you for the cards, care packages, taking care of my car service and for checking in on me. I am very fortunate to work with a team that cares as much as all of you.

Olivia & Will,
I hope you enjoy
this book. Denise O'Brien-Peters

"Keep your face always toward the sunshine –
and shadows will fall behind you."

–Walt Whitman

This book is dedicated to my loving husband Ron, and my sweet happy boy Zachary. Both of you have inspired me to be the best person, wife, and mother I can possibly be. Thank you for all of your love and support. You bring such happiness to my life!

TABLE OF CONTENTS

PREFACE

WRITING HAS ALWAYS BEEN MY THERAPY, MY WAY OF
expressing my emotions, my thoughts, and things I've learned.
When I was a little girl, I kept a diary. A small faux leather
cover, encased the little pages that documented my pre-teen
adventures. Early in life, I enjoyed writing. I always loved
hearing stories about old diaries, letters, and journals that
were discovered after many years. I wasn't envisioning I would
ever be compared to Anne Frank, but I found my freedom of
expression through writing. Growing up in a strict household
didn't provide a lot of opportunity to voice my thoughts or
emotions in a way I felt completely free. Therefore, writing
became my outlet. If I didn't have a friend to talk to, I would
take out my diary, or journal, and let my thoughts run freely
across the pages.

I vividly remember the time I found my diary had been
read. It was the first time I felt like I lost my freedom of
expression, and my freedom from being judged. It was hard
being a teenager who had no bedroom door, in a 100-year-old
farmhouse, having to walk through my brother's room to get to

my "Barbie-Colored" bedroom. If I had no privacy in my little square shaped room, and I couldn't express myself in my own little lined paper journal, what could I do? I knew, one day, I would recapture the feeling of freedom my journal provided.

I decided to write this book after I evaluated all the life-changing events that shaped me. I began to realize my life had many twists and turns, and with each one, I learned something significant about myself and about how to positively approach my life's challenges.

My hope is this book inspires others to find their inner warrior; the warrior that drives you to take control of the life you are given, and make the most out of every day. We all follow a different road to happiness. The path each of us chooses to follow, in order to reach our destination, determines whether we enjoy ourselves during the ride.

IT STARTS WITH FAMILY

I THINK OF MYSELF AS A SMALL TOWN FARM GIRL, who grew up thinking I had it *rough*, playing in the country, where my family raised every animal possible (pigs, cows, rabbits, sheep, but never horses). My dad is a modest farmer, who holds the title **"my hero"** based on two simple values: work ethic and modesty. There is not another man, or father, like him, and that is what makes him so special. Farming isn't an easy profession, and to know my dad is a farmer because he loves it makes all the difference in my world.

My mom is, and always has been a hard-working, intelligent, and passionate woman, who entered into motherhood at the ripe young age of eighteen. She had me first, followed three years later with my little sidekick of a brother, Tony. My parents worked hard for everything they have, and have never taken anything for granted. They earned everything on their own, through dedication and the support of family.

I probably wasn't the easiest child to raise. I always needed to be busy, and constantly pushed the envelope. In the O'Brien family, there is an antsy gene, which requires one to be moving at all times, or so it seems. As a child, there was always something else to be doing, something more to explore. I loved spending the summers visiting my grandparents, who lived one short, dusty, rock road mile from our house. My dad farmed several hundreds of acres near our home, and my mom worked thirty miles away, so my brother and I spent many summer days at my grandparent's house. My Grandma Mary took care of us while my dad and Grandpa Richard farmed.

My grandparents took us to church, after my parents decided they no longer wanted to attend Sunday services. My parents ensured we had a choice in religion. I knew there was some kind of "God," but I never really knew how to connect with what "God" was. I was raised to know right from wrong, and I knew there were consequences if I ever crossed boundaries, therefore, I thought I must have been doing something right since God never rattled the ground beneath me. I settled on "God is a mystery."

When people asked what my family farmed, the answer was, "whatever would grow and make money." That meant mostly corn and soybeans, but there was plenty of hay, wheat and several other things my dad chose to harvest for feeding cattle.

My dad was the only one of four children who chose to farm. His two sisters and brother opted for non-farming careers. When my dad talks about growing up as a kid, it is often like hearing about the perfect life of a farm kid; swimming in the pond, playing outdoors, riding and crashing bikes. He was an outdoorsy farm boy. I'm sure he found his own trouble, and probably kept many secrets to himself about what he actually did growing up as a country kid, but that is the great thing about my dad. He has his own fun and just lives life.

Grandpa Richard was just like my dad, only a few inches shorter. He had an orneriness about him that made him so fun. He loved his dark black coffee, and spent many mornings at the local coffee shop, with the other grubby farmers, exchanging stories about the price of corn, beans, and cattle. When Grandpa got a break from farming, often due to the change of seasons, or a storm coming in, he would always make time to entertain my brother and me. To this day, I remember Grandpa teaching me the proper way to win a game of croquet. Grandpa had a special way of *winning* most people didn't suspect. Croquet was the one game he was openly competitive about, and I enjoyed seeing that side of his personality. He wasn't one of those grandpas who felt the need to let the grandchildren win. He taught us winning can be fun, and his competitive spirit lives in us to this day. We just had to find the part of our competitive spirit that was a little greater than Grandpa's, if we wanted to beat him at any game. (We knew he cheated a little bit here and there, just to teach us a lesson about trying to beat him.) I'm not entirely certain how many Midwestern families play croquet, but the O'Brien's definitely know their stuff when it comes to yard sports, including lawn darts (before they made them less dangerous). Grandpa and Grandma also taught us every board and card game known. We played Rummy, Texas Rummy, Marbles, Checkers, Life, Pitch, Mastermind, Boggle, Pick-up

Sticks, and so many more I can't even remember. Pitch was a family competition. During our Thanksgiving and Christmas get-togethers, the entire family would break up into two groups. One group would play on the front porch, which was always a little chilly during that time of year. The other team got to play in the cozy kitchen. After an hour or two of playing, the losers from the front porch would play against the losers from the kitchen team. The winning front porch team competed against the winning kitchen team for the title of Winning Pitch Team. There were no medals. There was no money to be won. It was just simple family fun, and I loved it!

Grandma Mary made sure we were outside every day. Whether we were in the garden, picking vegetables, snapping beans, or simply checking out the newest addition to the family farm (baby chicks or baby calves), Grandma made sure we experienced farm living. We picked up freshly laid eggs, fed kittens, and helped weed the garden. If there was something to be done outside, we did it. In addition, Grandma loved to play the piano, and I loved to listen to her beautiful pieces from old tattered songbooks. Her fingertips rolled across the keys like feathers touching each ivory. She taught me how to sew, showed me how to bake using a real oven (not the easy bake kind), and when no one else wanted fresh green peas for dinner, she prepared them just for me. I was the oldest grandchild, and I always felt like grandma and I had a special bond. Grandma Mary is very special to me.

Grandma and my mom never really saw eye to eye, and for

the most part, it didn't cause any issues. However, one summer afternoon, my Grandma, my brother, and I were in her tiny farmhouse kitchen, and my brother said, "My mom doesn't like you." I'm sure he said it because Grandma asked him to do something he didn't want to. My brother was a little stinker when it came to respecting his elders. He didn't understand the saying, therefore he didn't follow the rule. I remember my Grandma remaining as calm as a cool, crisp cucumber, as she responded to my brother, "Oh she doesn't?" She wasn't shaken one bit by my brother's juvenile comment.

Several days later, my Grandma stopped by our house for a visit. In my mind, it was that day the stage was set, for the way my mom and Grandma would tolerate each other for years to come. My Grandma asked my mom about what Tony said, and the two of them had a little chat (far away enough we couldn't hear). From that point forward, everyone got along, but the family dynamic definitely changed. I, however, remained very loyal to my Grandma O'Brien. To me, she never did anything wrong, and she was my Grandma. I wasn't about to choose sides. In addition, my mom and I never saw eye to eye on things, which made establishing my position that much easier. Their strained, no love lost, relationship became the norm, and we all accepted it, as such.

My parents worked hard for everything they had, and instilled an invaluable work ethic in my brother and me. We both learned the importance of having a job, prior to turning sixteen. We knew we had to earn money to buy our own vehicles, gas, and insurance. My mom always said, "You'd better work hard now, because when you're eighteen, you are on your own." We knew she meant it. My mom was, and still is, anything but subtle when it comes to communicating. She tells it like it is and she doesn't expect a conversation in return. We found this out at an early age. Mom was the authoritarian of our household (and still is). She was a young mother, but she ran a tight ship, and she meant business. When she asked you to do something, you did it. If you asked why, she simply gave a look that said, "Don't ask me why, and just do it." There were consequences to be suffered if we didn't take care of the things we were asked to do. Mom always had a board, a flyswatter, or some other equally hurtful object she knew exactly how to use. She knew just the right way to make her point. My brother and I spent many years hiding several boards, coloring on them (as if the design would take away some of the pain that came with a swift whooping), and we broke many of them. We knew there was some power in teaming up on board hiding, but deep down, we both knew if we got a spanking, it was because we did something to deserve it (most times anyway). I'm sure it was a sign of the times, and looking back, kids were raised much differently than they are today. We were taught to be respectful of adults and of others, and my parents made sure we understood the importance of minding our manners. I'm certain it is why that is an important value to me today.

Tony and I played hard and it was great having a little brother to play with all of the time. We both did our own thing, but most of the time we participated in various activities together. During the wintertime, my mom told us to go outside and play in the snow, which resulted in us building the most memorable snow forts imaginable. In the summertime, we found fun in the sandbox. The sandbox was the location of our old chicken coop. My parents tore it down not long after the rooster decided to peck me and my dad took the rooster over the hill. Inevitably, my brother and I could find many ways to entertain ourselves, and also fight and bicker with each other along the way.

Mom grew up the second oldest of six kids, and from what I gathered over the last forty-one years, it was not an easy childhood. My mom's dad, Grandpa Shuman, was a military man. He served in the Air Force, and raised his six children on the core values of the military and strict discipline. Family has been the core of his existence and it is one of the things I respect and appreciate most about him. He tells stories about his travels throughout the United States, his time in the military, specifically the Mohave Desert, and he will debate with you about anything. Grandpa is usually never wrong. Just ask him. I am always amazed at how sharp he remains to this day. I could sit and talk to him about the price of gas for a good hour, and then continue on to other topics such as banking. Despite the fact he suffers from macular degeneration, it has not stopped him. He depends on my grandma to drive, otherwise, he is as independent and as set in his ways as ever. I think I would probably be set in my ways if I were eighty-four years old.

Grandma Shuman was always the one to give giant hugs

and smooches, and tell you she loves you, even when you were well past the age of needing a grandmotherly like squeeze (as if there would ever be a time when you didn't want that). If you closed your eyes and pictured what a grandma should look like, you would see her bright white smile, (albeit she could plop out those dentures at any time) beautiful blue eyes, and warm grandma-like glow. She has always been a terrific cook, preparing everything from fried chicken to the best holiday turkey and fixings. Her dishes could stand up to Paula Dean's any day of the week. They are just THAT good, and Grandma used just as much butter and lard as Paula Dean, too. It was always easy to see where my mom picked up her recipes, as well as her firm personality. Grandma was as sweet as a hot fudge sundae, until she was crossed. Then, she made it very clear that she was not "sweet little old Grandma."

I consider myself extremely fortunate to have gotten the opportunity to also know my great-grandparents from both sides of my family. It is rare nowadays for people to say they have any memory of their grandparents, but I feel especially blessed to have known my Great Grandpa and Grandma Walker and Great Grandpa and Grandma O'Brien.

LESSONS OF GROWING UP

BEING AN "ANTSY" CHILD AND TEENAGER BROUGHT forth some challenges, but mostly it drove me to do things better. My mom involved my brother and me in every sport possible. We began playing games when we were in kindergarten. Even though we lived ten miles from the closest town, mom drove us to and from baseball and softball practices and games. Mom ensured that Tony and I were involved in every extracurricular activity possible. My dad coached my brother's baseball teams, and mom was always in the stands cheering, filling the coach's ears full of "suggestions," and simply just being her supportive self. Tony and I both played sports through our childhood, teenage years and beyond. To this day, I believe it instilled a sense of commitment and dedication to being the best one can be at something, whether a team, individual sport or a profession. People count on you to show up to a game, be 100% focused, and ready to win. That is an extremely valuable lesson to learn at an early age. I have my mom to thank for making sure we stuck to what we started.

I attended college right after high school, and found my focus to be less about studying, and more about finding my freedom. My initial reason for attending college was to get out of Luray, Missouri, and away from my childhood. I wanted nothing more than to go out and prove I could be successful and make something of myself. After my first year, I changed universities, thinking I must have gone to the wrong "party school," but after two and a half years of mediocre grades, and two more schools, I knew I had done something wrong. Growing up in a farming community, with a high school graduating class of 75 students, made me want more. Unfortunately, class work wasn't my main priority. I was more interested in finding my own way to something better. (Whatever better meant, I didn't know.) I knew I was going to have thousands of dollars in student loans to pay, but I had no idea what I wanted do professionally. I always knew I would be on my own, and responsible for repaying my student loan debt. The thought of owing thousands of dollars was daunting. Especially, when I didn't really know what I wanted to be when I grew up.

After two years of sub-par grades, I moved back to my hometown, attended the local community college, and worked several retail jobs (in athletic sales, as well as women's clothing). The jobs were fun, and I met some very nice people. My mom would always ask, "When are you going to get a real job?" The question was a reasonable one to ask, but I thought I had a real job. I worked, got paid, and had money in my bank account. What was a real job? I knew I needed to figure things out relatively quickly, not only to please my parents, but also to establish some greater financial stability.

I got married at 21, and tried to fit into the local mold. After less than two years of being married, I decided life is not about compromising oneself, what you believe you deserve, or what you want to see in yourself. I got divorced and moved from small town Missouri to mid-sized Cedar Rapids, Iowa (or as my longtime friends like to call it, Cedar Stinky). Cedar Rapids was the home of Quaker Oats cereal mill (and I think it still is), and on any given day, one could smell cereal being made. The best day was always Cocoa Puffs day. The smell of chocolate could really kick start a day.

At twenty-five years old, I proclaimed my independence. I wanted nothing more than to excel professionally, travel the world, and meet new people. However, there was one thing that stuck with me...I needed to finish my degree and check the one item off of my list that constantly nagged me. I could hear my mom's voice saying, "When are you going to get a real job?" I knew I HAD to finish what I started, or I would never stop hearing that question. Sometimes you just have to quiet that voice inside your head. I was not at a point in my life where I could stop and put time into school. I was excelling at my job, performing well, and I was learning more about business management than I ever realized I wanted to know. This business management thing was for me. I made my next big jump to Chicago (the big Windy City).

In 2001, I enrolled in DePaul University and in 2003 and earned my Bachelor's degree while working full-time. The first thing I learned from my experience is attending a private Catholic university is very expensive. One must be fully prepared for the financial responsibility. However, the cost of the education rewarded me many times over with things money cannot buy. I met the most amazingly talented students of life, and developed relationships with friends that will last a lifetime. I have traveled to places I only read about as a child in National Geographic magazine and Encyclopedia Britannica (the Philippines, Hong Kong, Costa Rica, Spain, Venezuela, Greece, Italy, France, Mexico, just to mention a few). I knew with a Bachelor's Degree from DePaul University, I must have been moving in the right direction.

BEING VULNERABLE

I SPENT FIVE YEARS ON MY OWN LITTLE USA TOUR (Chicago to Charlotte, Charlotte to Boston) and decided it was time to move back to the place that felt most like home. No, I didn't move back to the farm. I moved back to Chicago. I missed the feeling of Chicago since the day I first moved there in 1999. I learned, while away, my happiest moments were with the friends and family I left.

After moving back, I quickly realized things were not as I left them, and discovered I had a lot of free time. I never had difficulty finding something to occupy my time, so that was not a problem. The problem was, I only had a couple of friends in the area now and they had their own lives, their own families, and very little extra time to spend with me. How could I expect my friends to drop everything and spend time with me, especially when I was the one who left town?

I explored several avenues of self-fulfillment, including meet-ups, mixers, shopping, extended weekend destination vacations, cocktail hours, and some occasional online dating. Many of the people I met were like me, and simply looking for others with similar interests. There was something missing from my personal equation, and I couldn't quite figure out how to meet people, like me, but different.

I shared my conundrum with my most real, raw, granola, "live your life on the edge" friend, Marnie. She suggested I try a new sport, triathlon. Marnie is the kind of woman and friend who lives on the edge of life. She takes chances and she inspires me to live outside of my comfort zone. I wasn't familiar with the sport, whatsoever. I knew it involved, swimming, biking and running, but how in the world I would learn to combine all three disciplines, into one, was a mystery. I became vulnerable! I entered into a new world, called multi-sport. I went out on a limb and joined the Leukemia and Lymphoma Society's Team in Training Program. I was always a runner, and loved being outdoors, so I thought I should give it a go. My first real race, with Team in Training, was the Steelhead Half Iron Triathlon, in August 2009. I raised money to help fight Leukemia & Lymphoma. My Grandpa O'Brien lost his battle with the disease several years prior, so supporting the charity meant much more than learning a new sport. It was my time to get uncomfortable, and do something much greater than myself. I had never raised money for a meaningful charity, so not only was I learning a new sport; I was learning how to involve others in my new commitment to help support a charity. I would help others fight a life threatening disease. The great part about Team in Training is everyone has one common goal, to support the charity. However, everyone is also there to meet new people, challenge themselves, and to compete. It was perfect for me, and exactly what I was looking for. The friendships I developed were some of the best I could have hoped for. I felt great about killing two birds with one stone... AND I met a terrific triathlon coach through the process.

My triathlon coach was fearless, and dedicated. All of the Team in Training athletes spoke highly of him. He was a two time Ironman Finisher and he was preparing for a third Ironman race in November 2009. That excited me. I was certain he must be made of steel. I had never met anyone like him. He was serious about his sport, serious about coaching, and was simply a no-nonsense man. The entire time I trained for the August race, I studied how he interacted with others, watched him train, and listened to what he said during training rides and runs. I started driving the thirty miles from the suburbs to the city, just to complete my swim training with the rest of the team. Somewhere along the way, I developed a little schoolgirl crush on my coach, and had to do something about it. I had to make sure he knew I existed. As the training weeks wound down, and race day approached, it was also time to celebrate my 39th birthday. Little did I know, Coach's birthday was eleven days after mine, and through the team, was invited to the Coach's birthday party.

On July 25, 2009, Coach noticed me. We can actually go so far to say that a fun night of celebrating two July birthdays turned into the beginning of something I never dreamed possible. I had met, dated, and even married before, but this man was not like the others. He spoke with purpose. He was gentle. His gorgeous blue eyes enveloped me every time we talked. I felt safe with him...but in a "let's go have fun kind of way." This was the type of man I had been yearning to meet for years. Oddly enough, I met him when I wasn't even looking... which made it even more special.

Coach Ron, and I started dating immediately, and it was easy. He called me every day. I never worried about what he was thinking, whom he was with, where he was going, or what he thought. If there was a God, I knew this man must have been specially selected for me. It was slightly scary, but in a fun and adventurous kind of way. The two of us enjoyed dinners together, talked about our families, shared family photos, and reminisced about our travels. He had biked through Italy, went on trips to Greece (to visit family), and was interested in exploring more of the world. This man was PERFECT for me! He was going to have to meet my family, but that would have to wait until after Ron completed his Ironman race in early November...which he invited me to attend as his very own race Sherpa.

I'd never witnessed an Ironman triathlon in person, so playing the role of "Sherpa," to my new triathlete boyfriend, was an adventure I was eager to pursue. I watched the World Championship race, televised from Hawaii, every year. That is the race everyone thinks of when they hear IRONMAN. I knew there would be a lot of intensity surrounding the race, but I had NO idea what it meant to be a triathlete's Sherpa...

not to mention my new boyfriend's Sherpa.

According to The Merriam-Webster Dictionary, a *Sherpa* is a member of a people who live in the Himalayas and are often hired to help guide mountain climbers and carry their equipment. My definition of an *Ironman Sherpa* is best summarized as a member of any people who can play a key role in helping an athlete have the best experience possible. An Ironman is a monumental goal, and when the day comes, it can be a bit overwhelming attending to all the travel, equipment, and logistics surrounding the event. Your job as support staff is exactly that: to support. Let your athlete take the lead, but be available to lend a hand whenever necessary. Easy, right?

Little did I realize, an Ironman race equates to an Ironman weekend. There are meetings to attend, packets to pick up, training to continue, gear and nutrition to prepare, people to see, and rest is required. Oh, and how could I forget about looking the part of the new girlfriend, without messing up something important for my triathlete boyfriend? Plus, Ron's mom would be there the entire weekend. Okay, so maybe a little pressure.

On November 22, 2009, Ron finished his third Ironman triathlon, with a race time of 12 hours, 6 minutes and 11 seconds. His own personal best! I was in complete awe of his commitment to making Arizona one of his best races, and so proud to see him accomplish his goal. This man was made of steel...and I couldn't wait to show him off at my family's Thanksgiving, in just a few days.

A THANKSGIVING
WE'LL NEVER FORGET

RON AND I HAD A COUPLE OF DAYS TO RETURN TO Chicago before driving to Missouri for the Thanksgiving weekend. The downtime was great for Ron, and he had an opportunity to let his body rest. I spoke with my parents and my brother about Ron, many times, and could not wait for them to meet him. Finally, I was bringing someone home to meet my family I felt they would approve. Getting my family's approval of things was a bit like playing a game of Jenga. I always had to think about positioning, strategy, and my next move, as they had an extremely short "trust leash." My brother used to tell all of the women he dated, "There are only three women you need to worry about in my life; my Grandma Shuman, my mom and my sister." For me, the approval process consisted more of my dad, my mom, and my brother.

During our drive to Missouri (only 5 hours from Chicago), I received a call from my brother, Tony. He and I had some serious discussions about his marriage in the prior weeks, and his call was to tell me that he and his wife were going to separate. The two of them had been struggling for several months, and they could not seem to figure out how to make it work. He was crushed! My brother was married once before, and had two beautiful girls from that marriage. Tony fought to get primary custody of his daughters, and after a few years of working to pull together all of the necessary information for a dad to have primary custody (one would think it would be easier), secured his right. Now, he was in a situation where he was going to need to take care of his two daughters, Keelie and Mackenzie, figure out how to share custody of his one-year-old son, Cameron, and work full-time. We talked about how we would figure it out. If there was one thing we O'Brien's always knew, we always had the support of our family to help us through the tough times, and this would be no different than any other time. I promised him I would help him in ANY way.

When Ron and I arrived at my parent's house, we spent time chatting with my parents, talking about Ron's race. Really, it was an opportunity for them to ask questions of him, and for him to take it all in. Ah, the fun of being in the hot seat. He took it all in stride and hit it off with my parents. My dad and Ron are both men of few words, however when they do speak, they have something important to say. My mom and I could ramble for hours, talking about lots of things, and have a perfectly meaningful conversation about nothing. After a few hours of small chat, we all called it a night (because we knew we had a big Thanksgiving meal the next day).

Early Thanksgiving morning, I asked my mom what Tony was going to be doing for lunch. I knew Keelie and Mackenzie were going to be with their mom, and given my conversation with Tony the night before, I assumed Cameron would be going with his mom to a family lunch. My mom wasn't entirely certain what his plans were, except to say he said he wasn't going to be doing anything for Thanksgiving. Well, if anyone knows our family, they know spending Thanksgiving alone is only an option if you are stranded on a deserted island. So, I called Tony to inform him Ron and I would drive down to Canton to meet him. I hadn't brought Ron all the way to Missouri to not meet my little brother. I left a message for Tony at around 9:30 a.m. to call me back so we could make plans.

At approximately 10:30 a.m., the Missouri State Highway Patrol knocked on my parent's front door. The trooper at the door was a colleague of my brother's, and knew my family. Tony graduated from the Missouri Highway Patrol 78th Recruit Class, and was an officer for eight years.

I listened, and watched, as if everything was being played in slow motion. Trooper Collier informed my parents, and me, that my brother had taken his own life, at 10:00 a.m. Thanksgiving morning. I watched my mom stomp through the room, devastated like a small child who just had her favorite baby doll yanked away. My dad was in shock. I froze. I could not have heard the trooper correctly. The look on Trooper Collier's face was all I needed to see to know I had heard everything correctly.

At that point, I frantically stumbled through the house, trying to find Ron. Holy Shit! This was supposed to be a weekend of family time, giving thanks, and home prepared dishes. My mind could not process everything. I went from one end of the house to the other, and became convinced I lost Ron (even though my parent's house is not big enough to lose a person). I soon realized he was in my dad's bathroom, showering. I walked in, bent over on my knees, and somehow, spoke the words I never thought I would ever hear myself say, "Ron, my brother killed himself." Time stood still. Ron looked at me, stunned. Standing there in my dad's little green bathroom, Ron held me tight. I gasped, trying to breathe; feeling like someone was sitting on my chest. Ron didn't know what to say. He was in shock by what transpired. He just met my parents the prior night, and was planning to meet the rest of my extended family that day, AND my brother took his life. I was completely confused and in shock, but I cannot begin to imagine how he must have felt, thrown into this unfathomable situation.

Nothing made sense! It couldn't possibly be true that Tony, my brother, the big, tall, strong, seemingly invincible State Trooper and Marine, would do something like this. His best friend, David, took his life in 1999. Tony and David grew up like brothers, and it devastated him when David chose that path. In addition, my family experienced two suicides, one in 2006, and the other in 2008. My uncle James took his life while living in Oklahoma, and then my cousin Brian did the same. How in the world could a family go through three suicides in three and a half years? It wasn't possible.

What unfolded in front of us was a story which will replay in my mind for the rest of my life. It's a story with many missing pieces, and one my family has tried to wrap their minds around for over four years. My brother loved his children more than life itself, and because of that, his death will never make sense to us. His daughters and his son brought him so much joy. Tony loved being a dad, and wanted nothing but the best for them. It tears me up to think about the things his children will never get to experience. I think about the first father-daughter dance my nieces will not get to enjoy, or the special father-son hunting trip Tony would love to have shared with Cameron. The sadness that comes with these things is not easy to comprehend.

Losing my brother was one of the most devastating experiences I have ever endured. I looked up to my younger brother, and respected him for reasons he never knew. He decided early on he wanted to join the Highway Patrol and become a State Trooper. Everything he did was to prepare himself to achieve his goal of completing the academy and earning a spot within the ranks of the Patrol. My dad was the only other person I knew who pursued what he wanted in life, and Tony made me think about what I was passionate enough to want to do for the rest of my life.

I remember a few days after Tony passed. Ron and I had returned to Chicago so I could get clothes and return to Missouri. After packing a bag of appropriate funeral clothing, I went for a short neighborhood jog. Running has always been my stress release, and I have found my most peaceful moments when I am outside, taking in the fresh air and allowing my mind to be free. I recall getting about a half mile down the street, and abruptly stopping at the corner. I looked up, and the sky was the most beautiful blue color I had ever seen. My eyes swelled with enormous tears, and all of the sadness poured out. I couldn't hold the emotions in any longer, and I spoke to the sky. I told Tony, whom I believed was somewhere up there, how mad I was. After several minutes, standing there alone, having my gut wrenching conversation, I turned around and ran back home. It was a short run, but a necessary break I desperately needed. When I walked into the house, Ron greeted me in the hallway between our front entryway and kitchen. He could see I was crying, and he reached out and held me. It immediately reminded me of the hug he gave me when I told him the news about Tony. He held me for what seemed like five minutes, and assured me we would get through everything together. I was blown away by the commitment he was demonstrating, especially considering we had only been dating since the end of July. This man was the one I had searched for my entire dating life. How ironic he entered my life at a time when I needed him the most.

Not long after our embrace, I started one of my few trips back to Missouri, preparing for my brother's funeral, and being with my family. Tony passed away on November 26th, 2009, and the visitation and funeral were not until December 1st. Those days seemed to be filled with such sadness. I was in Missouri without Ron, and while it was getting colder outside, I filled my time with running. I ran up the dirt road and up the rock road several times during my stay. The time outdoors gave me the opportunity to clear my mind, cry and to try to make sense of what happened. The gravel road became my escape, as it was for many years growing up. I spent many years of my life going up and down the gravel road to my grandparent's house. I used to run away to the bridge connecting my parent's and my grandparent's houses together at the halfway point. The bridge is no longer there, but it held many memories of my childhood. I wrote my boyfriend's name on the bridge, I rode the four-wheeler in the mud below the bridge during the summers. The bridge was my sanctuary.

While I tried to comprehend everything that happened, I knew I needed to allow myself to be in the moment and there was nothing I could do but comfort my family.

I've read about the phases of grief and loss, and moved in and out of each phase as if on a lifetime five-ride pass at the amusement park, "Not So Great America." Welcome aboard the Denial Isolator. Now, let's move to the Anger Train. Oh, don't forget a stop at the Depression Session. Before departing the station, be sure to whiz by the Bargaining Cyclone, before entering the Acceptance Tunnel.

For three years, I was angry, hurt, and just plain pissed off and disappointed in my brother. He took something from my nieces and nephew that should have never been taken from them. He took "the world is a beautiful place" glasses off, crushing them like they were meaningless pieces of plastic junk from the local dollar store. Yet, when I hear the kids talk,

I hear them recall the fondest memories of their dad. Keelie has the most memories, because she was ten when he passed. Mackenzie was only six, and she asks questions about what it was like growing up with her dad. Cameron was only one year old when Tony passed, so he will never know what it was like to have Tony as a father.

Over the last year, I have come to accept that my brother's mind was in a place I will never know or begin to understand. For me, time has helped ease the pain of his loss, but time also makes me miss him even more. How could I go from talking to him on the phone during almost every car ride, to not speaking to him once in four years? I will always find humor in the "Tonyisms" he conjured up from movies, or stories he told about the characters he came across in his job. His laugh was infectious, and his stories hilarious. He could talk the hind leg off of a donkey without trying, and he was the biggest bullshitter I have ever known. One thing I loved most about him was he was a no-nonsense guy. He stood for what he believed in, and you always knew where you stood with him. He didn't mince words if he thought you were full of crap, and he didn't play games. I'll never forget him telling me I didn't have any place telling him how to parent his kids, since I didn't have any of my own. We disagreed on that point, but he knew I was the best aunt to his children. I respected my brother and was proud of him, and disagreements were like water under the bridge in our family. He loved being a Missouri State Highway Patrol Trooper and had such respect for his fellow Troopers, and his Commanding Officers. The impact my brother had on others was very evident at his visitation and funeral. I have never seen so many men in uniform, community members, family, and friends paying tribute to a one-of-a-kind man, my brother. Hundreds of patrol cars lined the highway in front of the funeral home. There were officers who drove from the main headquarters in Jefferson City, many who came from all over the state of Missouri, and of course the local officers who worked with my brother daily. That cold December 1st day is one I will forever remember as a time of extreme sadness, but also, one of pride. Fellow officers, military brotherhood and so many people within the community respected my brother.

I have researched a lot about suicide over the past few years, and found peace with what happened to Tony. I will never understand it, nor will I ever be able to explain it to anyone. I have simply come to accept my brother chose to do something at a time when he wasn't in his right state of mind. I was not in his mind, nor do I know what he was dealing with emotionally and or mentally. I simply have to accept the fact that our family must move forward with positivity and purpose. The community has helped with fundraisers for the children's educations, and everyone keeps an eye on how they are doing. There is love and support all around, and I believe that will make the difference. As long as I am on this earth, I will see to it they know all of the stories about their dad, teach them things I think Tony would have wanted them to know, and most importantly, love them unconditionally.

My parents have changed as a result of my brother's death. Things in life are different for them now. My parents get all three kids every other weekend, from both of my brother's ex-wives, and that is how they will grow up knowing one another. Their roles as grandparents shifted to playing the role of a parent in some way. They are filling the role my brother is not around to fulfill, and in doing so, they are making sure the kids know what it means to grow up as a family. It has not been an easy road for anyone, but I am so proud of my parents for how they have stepped up, kept peace when it wasn't easy, and focused on the kids. They have made a commitment to be there for the children at all times, and in doing so, I believe it has helped the children know their family is going to take care of them, no matter what the situation.

I soul searched after going through the devastating and traumatic loss of my brother. I became obsessed with making sure his children had a role model they could look to for strength and encouragement. I have never shied away from being a role model, but I felt an extra sense of urgency, ensuring the kids could see you simply do not give up in life. To me, it was important for the kids to know you push harder, and you do things that make you stronger. You never give up!

My brother Tony

ANYONE CAN BE AN IRONMAN

WATCHING RON TRAIN FOR, AND PARTICIPATE IN AN Ironman triathlon had such a positive impact on me, that I thought competing in an Ironman would be a great way to push my mental, emotional, and physical self through the loss of my brother, and at the same time, show the kids what their Aunt Denise was all about. In 2010, I signed up for the 2011 Ironman Wisconsin race.

Signing up for an Ironman triathlon is the easy part. Training for the 140.6 mile race is the hardest part of the entire equation. When I signed up for Ironman Wisconsin, I already had some insight into the amount of time it would require preparing for such an event, because I watched Ron go through the training. Getting oneself ready for Ironman training requires a great deal of planning and mental preparation. Thank goodness, Ron agreed to do the race with me. I knew he would play a critical role in getting through the emotional, mental, and physical components of the training and the race. He successfully completed the Wisconsin race twice, so I knew he could help me achieve my goal.

Ron became my partner in life. In November 2010, he proposed. November 2009, was such a terrible month the proposal breathed new life into both of us. I am convinced, many men would have bailed on a relationship if they went through what we did with my brother's passing. Ron wasn't that kind of guy. He showed me he was my partner through the good times and bad. Not once did he get scared or speak of our relationship being too difficult.

We were excited to start a life together, and what better way to get ready for a wedding than to train for a race. We decided to get married in January 2012, to give ourselves enough time to enjoy the engagement, train and complete the race, and then have a few months before the wedding. Looking back, I should have realized, Ron and I would go through life in a "live life to the fullest" kind of way. I don't know too many people who train for, and compete in an Ironman, and plan their wedding at the same time. We did, and it worked!

The actual training for a September race begins in January, with an assumed base training beginning in the November to December timeframe. All time considered, one is actually training for approximately ten months. In the beginning, the training is about building a base (including developing strength, establishing a nutrition regimen, and ensuring one's body is able to get through a good workout with relative ease.)

Starting on January 31, 2011, every day, but one, was filled with swimming, biking and running. A typical day would consist of the following schedule:

START OF TRAINING SCHEDULE	
Monday	Swim 60 minutes, run 30 minutes
Tuesday	Bike 60 minutes, strength/core exercise for 30-45 minutes
Wednesday	Swim 60 minutes, run 30 minutes or REST
Thursday	Bike 60 minutes
Friday	Swim 60 minutes
Saturday	Run 60 minutes
Sunday	Bike 75 minutes

This schedule continued, with gradual increases in the training times and intensity levels, over a 32-week period. The longest week of training was the week of August 22nd.

Monday	Swim 120 minutes continuous (3500 meters+), run 60 minutes
Tuesday	Bike 90 minutes, strength/core 35 minutes
Wednesday	Swim 60 minutes, run 60 minutes
Thursday	Bike 60 minutes
Friday	REST/stretch
Saturday	Run 18 miles
Sunday	Bike 112 miles, run 15 minutes
END OF TRAINING SCHEDULE	

Training for an Ironman, or anything you want to do well, requires time, and commitment. That is what is so terrific about the sport of triathlon. The people I met are all busy, committed professionals, just like me. Somehow, they all find ways to make the time to train and race, while having fun with friends from the triathlon community. It isn't just a sport, it's a family. Some may refer to it as a crazy family.

One of the most challenging parts of training is when you are not training. Your body goes through so much preparation, that when the training schedule is reduced, it's like being tapered off of a drug (if I were to imagine being on drugs). I remember feeling antsy, nervous, fidgety, irritated, and just plain ready to race the two weeks prior to race day, September 11, 2011. Ron told me stories about his taper weeks, and I thought he was crazy. He told me how he could not be around crowds of people, and he felt antsy all of the time. The feeling of crawling out of one's skin could be equated to Ironman tapering. I experienced, first hand, what he had explained. If I felt like this two weeks before race day, what was I going to feel like on race day?

Race weekend was exciting. We trained hard for Ironman Wisconsin, and we were ready. Our friends were racing with us, other friends were there to cheer us on, and our families were in town to share the weekend activities. To this day, I believe an Ironman spectator has an incredibly challenging job. They spend their entire day outside, cheering for their chosen athlete or athletes. They are up at the crack of dawn to find the perfect spectator location for the "every man and woman for themselves" swims. Once the swim is over, they set out in search of the ideal spot to watch the bike, which really entails seeing their athlete for a few brief minutes as they pass. After the first pass, there is an hour, or sometimes two before they pass again. Lastly, the marathon is the most fun for a spectator, as it is the last leg. Even then, there can be 4-5 additional hours of waiting.

For me, one of the most exciting parts of the entire Ironman race is hearing those four marvelous words spoken by Mike Riley, "You are an Ironman." There is no other feeling like it. Being in a state of motion for over fourteen hours causes your body to endure some tremendously painful experiences, like cramping legs, and having very little control of your body accepting foods and liquids. I learned early on to listen to my body, and not to overextend myself. My goal was to finish the race, and that is exactly what I did. Mike Riley may have told everyone else I was an Ironman, but I knew acquiring the title was much more than hearing him say it. It was about the journey along the way.

People have commented completing an Ironman race is something they could never do. Truth be told, anyone can complete an Ironman. It simply takes dedication and commitment to something. In varying ways, we are all Ironman Finishers, regardless of completing 140.6 miles of swimming, biking, and running. When I think about the people I have met in my life, many of them have completed their own type of Ironman. It could have been having a baby against all odds, a downhill skiing competition, or working a 14-hour day in the fields, trying to get crops planted before a storm rolled in. Saying I completed an Ironman Triathlon makes me feel proud of my accomplishment, but more proud of my dedication to something very meaningful in my life. The idea of quitting never crossed my mind, and as far as I am concerned, quitting is a word I have chosen to eliminate from my vocabulary. If something was ever worth starting, then it is definitely worth finishing.

Ironman Finisher

THE PERFECT START

TRAINING FOR A VERY LARGE TRIATHLON TAKES A significant amount of time, and if you think that's hard, try planning a wedding. All we knew was we wanted our closest family and friends to celebrate our special day. However, I didn't want to spend the time on all of the planning and negotiating that comes with a wedding. We decided to hire a wedding planner. While not the J.Lo one might envision from the movie "The Wedding Planner," we absolutely loved Laura. She took care of everything for us, and she made the planning process incredibly easy.

Initially, I wanted a destination wedding. Ron reminded me how many family and friends we wanted to include, and after several planning discussions and multiple bottles of wine, we agreed, a Chicago based wedding would be the best option. The cost of a wedding is normally ungodly, and when you take into account the Chicago cost factor, you end up with a few options for having a reasonably priced wedding. Ron and I landed on a January date. We could reduce our costs significantly by having it in an off month. We both loved Italian food and wine, so we chose a warm and inviting restaurant in downtown Chicago, called Salvatore's. If you hadn't heard of Salvatore's, you would have no idea where it was located. That was one of the great things about it. Most people didn't know where it was located, and it was quaint and cozy – very Ron and Denise.

Luckily, January 28th was somewhat mild. It was a "thirty-ish" degree-day, and there was only a little bit of snow on the ground. The ceremony lasted approximately 20 minutes, was officiated by one of our good friends, and we were joined by our closest family and friends.

Ron's sister and her children flew in from Europe, many members of my family came in from Missouri, and my friends from North Carolina, Massachusetts, Arizona and Virginia all attended. Ron and I decided combining the ceremony and reception into one location would be ideal for everyone. It would lessen the burden of having to go between the wedding and reception, and it would make it very easy for us to decide on what type of ceremony to have. Given neither of us had settled on a church, or religion, we wanted to include in our ceremony, we asked one of our very good friends to officiate. Who better to conduct the ceremony than someone who knew both of us, knew how Ron and I met, and watched our relationship come together. The most memorable part of the day was the feeling I was starting a new chapter of life with my best friend, and the love of my life. I had not expected to find a man who loved me despite all of my idiosyncrasies and very dry sense of humor. I felt like I became an entirely different person, a better person, with Ron by my side.

Many things in my life changed when Ron entered my life. I previously came to the conclusion I might become the little old lady who lived in a house, all alone, with 20 cats. Fortunately for me, I am allergic to cats, so I could eliminate the option from the possibilities. To this day, I know Ron and I were on parallel paths in life. We got very lucky when our paths converged in Chicago, the place we both love. It is very true when they say everything happens for a reason. There was a reason I moved back to Chicago, a reason why I took a risk and got involved in triathlon, and a reason why Ron was in my life. We belonged together. We complimented each other and we were better people with one another.

Ron brought me into the Team in Training triathlon family. I brought him into my world of diverse friendships, developed while living in different cities and traveling to different countries. Our wedding day was absolutely perfect with all of these people included.

We enjoyed dinner, dancing, visiting with our friends and family, and then left for the airport at 11:00 p.m. The next morning, we flew to Hawaii. It was the perfect start to our life as a newly married couple.

Newlyweds

LIFE IS MEANT TO BE LIVED

DURING OUR FIRST YEAR OF MARRIAGE, RON AND I agreed we would not sign up for any major races, and we would just enjoy our first year as newlyweds. We trained so hard the prior year, all we really wanted to do was have fun with friends, family, and travel.

I was going to turn forty in July, so it was a perfect time to catch up with my fabulous friend, Jen. She and I were turning forty within a few months of each other, and decided to take a trip to St. Thomas, USVI. The two of us traveled together several times before, and had many fun memories that will last a lifetime. We could travel anywhere together, and always come home with plenty of hilarious stories like; missing our bus stop in Mexico and riding through the non-touristy areas of Cancun, almost missing our flight out of Mexico, and Jen dropping a shirt in the toilet after too many "buy one get one free" Chi-Chi's at the pool happy hour. The laughs were always guaranteed, and the love for each other was something I envisioned two sisters sharing. I didn't have a sister, but if I did, I know she would be just like Jen.

The trip to St. Thomas was exciting from the beginning. Thanks to my extensive list of food allergies, I experienced an allergic reaction to a granola bar as we made our way from the airport to the hotel. The moment I got out of the transport van, I told Jen I needed to use the restroom (leaving her with my suitcase and the responsibility of paying the driver). She didn't think anything of it, she was well aware of my bathroom issues. As I made my way to the hotel restroom, I became dizzy, nauseous, and knew I needed to get the granola bar out of my system. (Yes, vomiting was something I had grown accustomed to.)

Just as I found the women's restroom, I felt the need to sit down. I found the nearest wall and eased myself down to the floor. I knew this wasn't going to be good. I was in excruciating pain. I felt the pain in my abdomen and through my lower back. I had been diagnosed with eosinophilic esophagitis (yes, that is really how it is spelled) a few years prior, and something in the granola bar was causing an allergic reaction, thus, forcing my digestive system to seize up. The pain was all too familiar, and I knew the only solution was to avoid certain foods, and if I accidentally ate something, (I wasn't aware I was allergic to) I had to get it out of my body. Unfortunately, the reaction was severe, and I did not have enough time to purge my body of the evil allergen. Thank God, a couple was sitting on a couch close-by and saw I was having a problem. The woman happened to be a nurse, and identified my vitals were elevated. My heart was racing, I was panicking, and Jen had no idea I was around the corner causing a scene. Within a short amount of time, the hotel emergency personnel were by my side, asking questions, trying to identify the issue. I advised them I was carrying an Epi-pen in my purse, and needed a shot. Within seconds, they stabbed my thigh and I started to feel the pain subside. Again, thank God, someone saw I was having a reaction and called for help. It was more proof that God works in mysterious ways.

The excitement of the moment passed, and Jen and I continued with our vacation, as if nothing ever happened. We spent our days lounging by the pool, playing bingo and drinking $2 Peroni's, kayaking through mangroves, and snorkeling with beautiful sea life, including majestic sea turtles. During the trip, I told Jen that Ron and I were not trying to have children, but we were leaving it up to the powers that be. Ron and I decided we spent so much time going through life alone that when we did meet each other, we were just happy experiencing life together. If children were meant to be in our future, we would not put unnecessary pressure on our relationship, and see where the future would take us.

In the month of October, Ron and I took our first trip together to Napa Valley and Sonoma. I had been to wine country with my girlfriends, but Ron and I thought it would be a great trip to enjoy as a newly married couple. We had the most memorable trip to California. The time in Napa Valley was unforgettable. We took advantage of hiring a driver for one day, who coordinated an amazing wine tour of four different wineries and vineyards. We simply told him we enjoyed Pinot

Noir and Malbec wines. The rest was up to the driver. We left our wine tasting experience in the hands of someone who knew the area and would likely make the best recommendations. Our favorite winery ended up being named O'Brien Estate. The driver had no idea my maiden name was O'Brien, so it ended up being a very memorable experience.

The entire trip consisted of visiting five wineries, one of which I had been to with my girlfriends. VJB Winery was one of the Italian wineries that not only had some of the best wine, but they also had Italian foods available for purchase. One of the nice little treats was getting to sit in the outside courtyard and enjoy a wood-fired pizza. Pizza and wine could be two staples I might be able to live on forever.

One of our favorite trips-Napa

THE JOURNEY BEGINS

I HAVE COMPETED IN SEVERAL TRIATHLONS, 5K'S AND all of them required training and preparation. Without some type of endurance training, I would have been doomed for pregnancy. Ron and I got married when we were both in our 40's, and we agreed we would have children if it were meant to be. Sure enough, it was meant to be. We found out I was pregnant in November of 2012. After four at home pregnancy tests all showed the same results, we knew we were about to embark on a journey.

I am convinced women who say they love being pregnant are lying. There wasn't one part of pregnancy that made me feel beautiful or sexy. When I consulted with my previously, or currently pregnant girlfriends, they all confirmed they felt the same way. If your friends tell you anything different, feel thrilled for them, but be jealous.

Our baby was due on June 24th, and I decided to work as long as possible. I was able to work from home the last couple of weeks, so it made things easier. Friday, June 21st, I decided I could no longer actively participate in conference calls and work on projects because I felt like our son was practicing to be a soccer player for the Chicago Fire with all of his kicking. The baby's foot was always wedged in my rib cage and made sitting completely uncomfortable. I contacted my boss and informed him of my plan to start maternity leave on Monday. He agreed with my plan, and wished us well on our new endeavor. Fortunately, I have one of the coolest bosses around. He has four children of his own, so he gave me better advice than some of my girlfriends.

My husband and I are both very punctual, so when the doctors told us our baby would likely be early, we were thrilled. Nothing is worse than being late to the party. June 24th was just like any other Monday, except I was now on maternity leave and it was summertime. How could we have planned this pregnancy any better? My husband is a teacher, and off during the summer too. Score! The best part is we didn't plan any of it. We knew if we were meant to have a baby, it would happen at the right time.

At around 6:00 pm, Monday evening, I started to experience what is referred to as bloody show. Now, my husband will tell you that I tend to over share information with him, but I like to think of it as being all-inclusive. I thought he should verify what I was experiencing before I made a call to our OB (aka baby doctor). After doing that, we both agreed we should call the doctor. Sure enough, the doctor confirmed we should make our way to the hospital. The important thing to note is that the Chicago Blackhawks were playing in game six of the Stanley

Cup Championship Playoffs, so the timing of everything added a little extra excitement to our evening. The playoff series was 3-2 (Chicago leading) and game six was being played in Boston.

After a short twenty-minute car ride, we arrived at the Good Samaritan Birth Center. Lucky for us, we had an amazing nurse named Maria, who lovingly settled us in our room and showed us how to find the playoff game on television. We intently watched the game, awaiting a Chicago win, and sure enough, with 17 seconds to play, the Blackhawks won the Stanley Cup Championship. The newspaper headlines became the keepsakes for our baby boy, Zachary Allen Peterson.

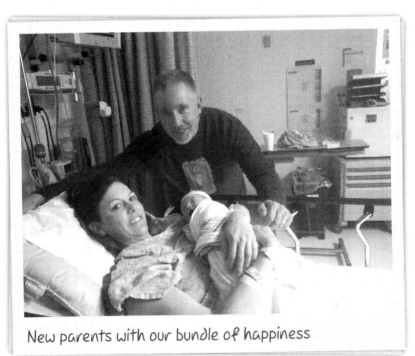

New parents with our bundle of happiness

After an exciting evening of Stanley Cup playoff action, spending several hours in labor, pushing with no success, then having to deliver via cesarean section, one becomes very tired. I remember the nurse asking if I wanted to hold Zachary, and my first thought was, "What if I drop him?" I could barely keep my eyes open, let alone think I might be able to hold my son. I suggested my husband hold our new baby and he gladly accepted. There are few things more amazing than seeing your husband hold his new son for the first time, and this vision is one of my favorites of all time. The glow on Ron's face is one that will forever be stored in my memory.

On Friday, we were released from the hospital, and finally able to take our little family home. As first-time parents, we were anxious to go through all of the first-time things the nurses made seem so easy. What if we forgot something? What if we didn't know how to handle a situation? What if we didn't feed him enough? What if we fed him too much? What if we couldn't master the art of the swaddle? All of these questions, and many others, came to mind as we made our way home.

The first night was a little tough, especially since Zachary wanted nothing to do with his crib. We figured out, quickly, my husband and I could not be awake at the same time and be able to effectively manage taking care of a new baby. We decided it would be easier if we worked in shifts. We opted for using formula, so it was reasonable both of us could manage feedings at different times.

Saturday was a new day, and my mother-in-law was going

to be visiting. The wonderful thing about having a baby is everyone wants to visits. In order to see the baby, people bring you food. This is especially great because the last thing you want to worry about is cooking dinner. Not only is my mother-in-law a great cook, she is a doting grandmother, so this meant she would want plenty of doting time with her grandson. Translation...a little break for us.

During dinner, I remember looking at my husband on a couple of occasions, and feeling slightly "off." I recall thinking that something didn't seem quite right, but chalked it up to postpartum hormones. In the back of my mind, I worried about these hormones, mostly because of the fact, my brother committed suicide. I never wanted to be in a position where I wasn't in control of my emotions or myself, and I knew our family history all too well. After we finished dinner, I felt fine and thought the pain medication must be causing the slightly "off" feelings. I heard stories about Norco, and never was a fan of taking any kind of pain management narcotic.

The next day started like the previous few days. I was a new mom, and my husband and I were managing our lives around an entirely new schedule. Despite the fact I had a cesarean section, I knew I needed to help take the dirty clothes to the basement laundry room. I could not wrap my mind around the idea I should "take it easy" and ask my husband to take on more duties. After putting the laundry in the wash, I decided to get myself ready for the day. We were expecting family visitors at noon, and I needed to get myself showered and presentable.

After showering, I was standing at the sink, preparing to brush my teeth, and froze. I was holding my toothbrush in hand, staring to my left, and I was stuck in time for what seemed like a lifetime. I knew something wasn't right, but I couldn't say anything, and I couldn't move. I stood in front of the mirror, helpless, thinking to myself, "I need to yell for Ron." After a minute or two, I was able to yell for my husband, and he came upstairs to find me upset and afraid. I told him something was wrong, but I couldn't explain what happened when I froze with my toothbrush in my hand. We both thought I must have overextended myself. I just carried a load of laundry to the basement, and I also just steamed up the bathroom with a warm shower. I had placed the Napa cabbage in my bra, as my OB had advised, and Ron thought maybe I was having a reaction to the cabbage. Considering my track record, it was not unusual for me to have allergic reactions to healthy food items. We decided it was best for me to lie down and relax for a few minutes before doing anything else.

After ten to fifteen minutes of resting, I felt a little better and got myself dressed and ready for our afternoon visitors. As I was walking down the stairs, my husband asked if I was feeling better, and I responded with, "I don't know." I walked to the trashcan, to throw something away, and suddenly felt myself freeze again. Ron was saying things to me, like, "Denise, talk to me" and "Denise, say something," but all I could do was focus on what was on my left side. I felt like I could only look to the left, and then my left hand started to twitch. Ron immediately called 911, and within a very short period of time, the ambulance was at our home. The paramedics stuck me with a needle and began taking my blood. At the same time the ambulance arrived at our house, my husband's family arrived. Not a great way for them to meet Zachary for the first time. I could see the fear on Bernie's face, as she was in a similar 911 situation Father's Day weekend. She had recently undergone heart surgery and it seemed, this situation was hitting too close to home. I was lying on the couch, panicking, and again, my mind went to my brother. What if there was something wrong with me that would cause me to harm myself? It couldn't be possible. I wanted nothing more than to start a new chapter of my life with my husband and my new baby.

Within a very short period of time, I was whisked away to the nearest hospital, thinking the whole time, please let things be ok. This was not the new motherhood journey I envisioned.

WE MUST HAVE MADE A WRONG TURN

WHEN I ARRIVED AT THE HOSPITAL EMERGENCY room, I was evaluated, asked a lot of questions, and eventually had a CT scan. Keep in mind, I had just come home from the hospital two days prior, and was recovering from a C-section. The last thing I expected to be doing was spending time in an emergency room.

After evaluating the CT scan, the doctor informed us that an MRI was ordered. I would be taken back to the MRI area as soon as possible. Unfortunately, I am claustrophobic, so the combination of an MRI and claustrophobia do not go well together. Fortunately, there are drugs (Ativan) that help people like me. I was given a dose of Ativan prior to the MRI, which proved to be beneficial for all involved.

I couldn't tell anyone how much time passed from the point I returned from the MRI area until we were visited by a neurosurgeon, but the key point is we were visited by a **neurosurgeon**. The emergency room doctor had identified a mass on my brain from the CT scan, and as a result, the neurosurgeon was contacted. Now, when someone tells you there is a mass on your brain you think to yourself, "holy shit." But when someone tells you there is a mass on your brain and there is a neurosurgeon who will be reviewing your MRI results, you think to yourself, "Holy shit, am I going to die?"

Dr. Rabin met with my husband, our newborn son, and me as soon as the MRI results became available, and I remember him pulling up the images on the screen. His most memorable comment was, "wait for it." We reviewed the images of my brain, and initially, everything looked like one would expect a brain to look. As the images were displayed, we saw a white mass appear and continue to grow in size. This was the "wait for it moment" the doctor mentioned. As we continued through the images, we ended up seeing a large tumor 4.8 x 3.9 x 4.6 cm (about the size of your fist), referred to as a meningioma. Now, it's never comforting to hear the word tumor, and it is especially not comforting when you hear it is a large tumor. It's especially nerve wracking when your tumor is called a meningioma. How in the heck do you spell that? Many things went through my mind. I started questioning why we hadn't created a will. I wondered if I would be around to celebrate my son's first birthday. I began questioning why God continued to put me through things like my brother's suicide and now a brain tumor. We were told the tumor was likely benign, which made us feel much better. Additionally, Dr. Rabin assured us that it could be worse.

My husband began researching meningioma's as soon as we got the diagnosis. Once we started reading about it, we quickly started to gain more insight into how many people are diagnosed with brain tumors every year. I was shocked! Webster's Dictionary defines meninges and meningioma as follows:

Meninges (meh-NIN-jeez) *The three thin layers of tissue that cover and protect the brain and spinal cord.*

Meningioma (meh-NIN-jee-OH-muh) *A type of slow-growing tumor that forms in the meninges (thin layers of tissue that cover and protect the brain and spinal cord). Meningiomas usually occur in adults.*

Despite the fact we just had a baby, were just told I had a brain tumor, and would need to share the stressful news with our families, my husband and I kept our wits about us. I was admitted to the hospital as soon as soon as we confirmed the results of the MRI. The neurosurgeon wanted to reduce the swelling of my brain prior to surgery. June 30th became the beginning of the next adventure in our newlywed lives. Yes, we were newlyweds. We had gotten married on January 28, 2012, and a year and a half later, we had a new baby and a tumor. On July 8th, I would undergo surgery to remove the meningioma, and on July 14th, I would hopefully be home to celebrate my 41st birthday.

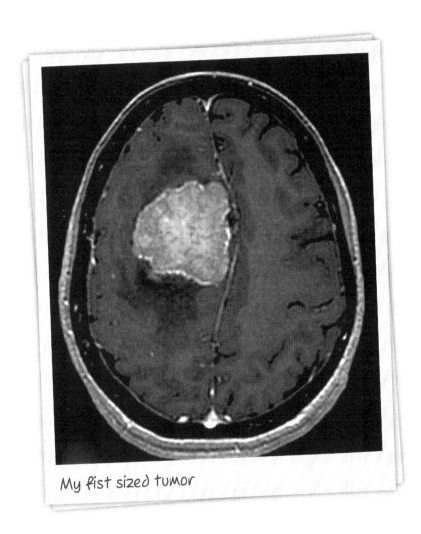

My fist sized tumor

NEW MOM WITH A BRAIN TUMOR

WHEN THEY TELL YOU THAT YOU ARE GOING TO HAVE to be in the hospital for eight days prior to brain surgery, (after you've just had a cesarean-section), they should also say you are going to be poked, prodded, stuck, drugged, questioned, and tested beyond belief. Not only are your emotions tested, because you just had a baby, but also because you were just told you have a brain tumor.

My first night in the hospital was an interesting one, as I was in the Cardiac ICU section. I was given a serious cocktail of drugs, including: Norco (from the C-section), Ativan (the "help me not freak out during this MRI" drug), Decadron (steroid), and Keppra (anti-seizure). One of the ingredients in my drug cocktail was causing issues with ringing in my ears, and I was in a whole other world of relaxation. I remember very little about my first night in the hospital, except for the fact that my drug cocktail caused me to heckle a poor pregnant nurse who was assigned to me. I could hear her speaking to someone on the phone, trying to get things moving along since my admission, and I was cheering her on as she was having difficulty getting things she needed. I was saying things like, "Yeah let them have it. Tell them who the boss is." The poor woman probably wondered what kind of psychiatric patient she was assigned to. In addition to cheering on the nurse, I later found out I fell asleep while my sister-in-law was saying a prayer to me over the phone. I don't know if she ever really knew I fell asleep, but I believe God forgave me. If there was one thing I knew, it was I now needed to believe in something greater than myself. I couldn't keep thinking God didn't exist. When my brother died, I seriously contemplated how any supreme being could allow something so tragic to happen. Over time, I came to understand my brother was in a different place than I will ever be, so whether it was a Catholic God or any other force, I had to put my faith in the power of something.

The next day was better, as my meds were working, and my ears were no longer ringing. The neurosurgeon wanted me to move as much as possible to ensure I didn't develop blood clots. This was great news for me, as I was not one to sit still. As I mentioned, the fidgety gene ran in my family, not to mention I remained relatively active throughout my pregnancy. During the ten months I was pregnant; I ran for the first five, and took daily walks around our neighborhood for the remaining five months. I wanted to keep the blood flowing, as well as prevent myself from having a nine-pound bambino.

Movement, in preparation for surgery, was a welcome prescription for managing nervousness. The nurses on the Cardiac ICU floor were encouraged by the number of times I made my exercise rounds. I was quick to let them know I was an Ironman Finisher, and I could do anything. Now, completing an Ironman triathlon was an entirely different challenge than taking on a brain tumor, but I was convinced the mental and emotional strength was the same for both. If I could train for a triathlon for nine months to complete a 2.4 mile swim, 112-mile bike ride, and 26.2 mile run (yes, a marathon), **and** I could prepare for a baby for ten months, I could definitely get through brain surgery as a new mom. No problem, right?

Eventually, I was moved to a different floor, with an equally wonderful view of downtown Naperville. You don't notice how beautiful things are until you think there may be a possibility of never seeing them again. Not only did I enjoy the downtown view, but I also appreciated the fact I had a private room to share with my continuous flow of visitors. It's truly mind blowing to think about how many people came to visit prior to, and after surgery. I tried to keep track of important daily learning's on an iPad Notes app. It was important to me to be able to share the story with our son, one day. He would never believe me if I didn't have pictures and notes.

My husband brought our son to visit every day. He was the extra ray of sunlight and happiness I needed. I was asked many times about postpartum, and each time I was asked, I responded with, "I feel just great!" How could I possibly feel anything other than elated? I just became a new mom, and nothing (not even a brain tumor) was going to take away my happiness. In addition, I had the most thoughtful and caring husband a woman could ever ask for. Ron was thrown into this crazy experience and not only was he doing his best to keep copious notes, but he was also trying to handle being a new father along with being a supportive husband to me (his newly diagnosed brain tumor wife). Somehow, Ron has always managed to amaze me with his strength and resilience. He contacted family and friends who could help take care of Zachary while he stayed with me many nights, he had an entire plan set up that allowed me to see my son, while also having ample time to rest. He knew I needed to see him and Zachary as much as they needed to see me. In addition, he kept my family updated and informed. He even helped coordinate a visit from my Aunt Kim and my two nieces.

Ever since my brother passed, I made sure my nieces and nephew knew they were a priority in my life. My nieces were scared when they learned about my tumor, but I assured them everything would be just fine. Seeing them prior to the surgery was not only an important visit for them, but it gave me the strength I needed to get through the next few days.

My two angels

APPRECIATE YOUR DOCTORS, NURSES AND TECHS

AS EACH DAY PASSED, I BECAME MORE AWARE OF JUST how much the doctors, nurses, and techs were doing for me to prepare for my upcoming surgery. Each day was different, and I had the benefit of meeting so many fabulous professionals. When friends asked me about how I liked my doctor, my standard response was, "Which one?" The truth was, I liked every single one of them, and felt fortunate I was "assigned" so many experienced and talented individuals. The nurses got me through each day, with their words of wisdom, their humor, and encouragement. A few nurses stood out to me, each for different reasons. One nurse, Laura, was one of the first to introduce me to the world of bedpan usage. When my pregnant nurse ended her shift, Laura got the 7:00 p.m. – 7:00 a.m. pleasure of dealing with my small bladder. I had never used a bedpan, but Laura helped me understand how to use one, and how to use it correctly. The first thing to know about using a bedpan is you cannot simply lie there and expect the pan to do all of the work. After a couple of times urinating on myself, I found that I needed to make some adjustments if this bathroom alternative was going to work. I eventually figured it out, and thankfully, (for both Laura and me) made it through everything with only a couple of mishaps. One of the happiest moments of my twelve-day hospital stay was hearing the doctor say I could stop using a bedpan and get up and use the bathroom.

The neurosurgeon visited my room at approximately 7:15 a.m., each day. My husband prepared for each morning's visit by having a list of questions we wanted answered. Dr. Rabin gave us detailed information, (as one would expect from an individual who is responsible for operating on brains) but what he did not realize is my husband was extremely thorough, wanting to understand everything involved in my medical procedures. Ron's list of questions turned into a notebook of questions, and by the end of the week, I'm sure the doctor probably wondered how he got so lucky to have two type-A personalities to deal with each day. On two occasions, my husband was lucky enough to accompany Dr. Rabin in the elevator. The poor man must have wondered why Ron was stalking him (it really was a coincidence Ron met him in the elevator.)

One of the interesting things about being in the hospital during the week of July 4th is that several doctors take vacation time. The neurosurgeon informed us he would be off for a few days, but another doctor would be doing rounds. He continued to inform us his backup was well equipped to monitor my progress and would recommend other tests if needed.

Our first encounter with the doctor started with a series of neuro checks. I was used to the neuro checks, because all of the doctors were completing daily checks. They started with having me squeeze the fingers on their hands, raising both arms (with my eyes closed) to a position known as "pizza box," raising my legs, lowering my legs, pushing my feet against their hands (like accelerating in a car), and a few other random checks. Well, this doctor had a few extra neuro checks up his sleeve. He reached into his pocket and pulled out, what appeared to be, two instruments from the 1970's. The doctor reminded me of Mr. McGoo and comparing him to the cartoon character helped me enjoy my time in the hospital. One instrument looked like a ravioli cutter, and the other some kind of tuning fork. After he received a positive reaction using both instruments, he pulled his keys out of his pocket and proceeded to run his car key along the bottom of my feet. I couldn't resist asking him, "Are you trying to turn me on?" Not only did my question mortify my husband, but it went way over the doctor's head, and I was the one left laughing at my own joke. How could I resist? This was the time to find humor in everything.

One of the other memorable doctors was the hematologist/oncologist. After my pregnancy, my OB indicated I had low iron. As a result, the hematologist checked my iron levels daily, and determined whether I was prepared for surgery. Unfortunately, my iron level was at 8.1, so Dr. B ordered daily iron supplements and an IV. The not so wonderful thing about iron is that it causes constipation. Oh, what a treat! I spent several weeks of my pregnancy constipated, so why not add insult to injury.

After a few days of iron, my iron level had increased to 8.8. I was encouraged by the improvement; however, my "stand in neurosurgeon" was concerned and ordered two units of blood. Fortunately, Dr. B agreed with the assessment and said it should prepare me well for surgery.

One of the reasons Dr. B was so memorable was his bedside manner. He went the extra mile to make me feel human. I didn't feel like I was just another patient needing care. I felt like he actually took the time to know me, and understand my family's needs. One of the nurses commented on her experiences with him, and re-enforced my feelings about his approach to patient care. When a nurse endorses a doctor, it means everything.

There is nothing like starting your Saturday morning with two units of blood being added to your body. I expected each unit to take approximately two hours to complete. To my dismay, each unit took approximately three hours to "download." The old saying, it's like watching paint dry, could easily be translated to, it's like watching blood drip. The process wasn't painful, so I was thankful they were using my sore IV stuck arm for a good reason. The next day, I learned my iron level went from 8.8 to 11.2. What a significant improvement. I was now prepared for surgery.

After completing my blood download, I was visited again by the entertaining doctor. He notified us he was pleased with my iron levels, and completed his daily neuro checks. He added a few new checks, including the drunk driving test (heel to toe), and walking on my heels and toes. After he left the room, he came back and asked me what the date was, as he did during every visit. He forgot to ask me earlier, and wanted to be sure I knew the answer. I'm not entirely certain if he realized the date was written on the dry erase board every day, but I simply answered the question.

Two days prior to surgery, we started to get more information about what we should expect on the morning of surgery. I was scheduled for an MRI at 5:30 a. m. The MRI would serve as the road map and be used by the neurosurgeon. He would be able to see the exact location of the tumor, and determine where to make incisions and cut my skull. Perhaps most people don't think twice when they are told their skull is going to be cut open, but I could not envision myself lying on the operating table with my skin peeled back, and a saw cutting my skull. If I ever thought about entering the medical field, I knew now I never wanted to participate in anything related to neurosurgery.

The night before surgery was more stressful than most days, except the day I was told I had a brain tumor. It became more real, more frightening, and more emotional. My parents were in town and enjoyed a Ted's Montana Grill dinner with us (via deluxe hospital room dining accommodations). After my parents left, my husband and I took a stroll through the floor halls. Walking the halls was a part of my daily exercise, and a form of mental and emotional therapy. Any type of forward movement always allowed me to clear my mind and remain focused on the task at hand.

Ron and I talked about how we were feeling, and got much

more in touch with the fact that we were both scared of the "what if" scenario. We talked about being scared days before, but it was so close to game time we both knew we had to be strong for each other. We talked about needing to make sure we had things in order for Zachary as soon as I got out of the hospital. When you are faced with your own mortality, you think of everything that needs to be taken care of so your child can have the best possible future. Although we talked about it before he was born, we had not gotten a will prepared. We had not established a college fund, and we had not discussed what would happen to the house since it was only in my name. These were all things we needed to officially have drawn up, but we would have to do that after surgery. I knew Ron and I were on the same page regarding Zachary's future, so there was no doubt if something happened, everything would be ok.

The days leading up to surgery were the first times, in my entire life, I ever considered the possibility of dying. That thought never had a reason to enter my mind. My goal was to enjoy my life to the fullest, and to share my experiences with my family and friends. Not once did I ever stop to think about what would happen if I didn't live to see my son grow up. But, the possibility slapped me in the face, and I could not ignore it. I was scared of possibility, but there was no way I was going to let a little brain surgery get the best of my spirit.

As Ron and I settled in the hospital room, embraced in an emotionally meaningful hug, a commercial loudly played Willie Nelson's song, "Always on My Mind." Ron and I looked at each other and exploded with laughter. The timing was perfect for such a sappy, yet meaningful song. Thanks to Willie, Ron and I settled in for the night with bit of laughter on our minds.

Before going to sleep the night before surgery, we had one final meeting with my nurse. She was one of the most thorough health care professionals I met. If there was one nurse, who could have specifically been chosen for me, it was her. We walked through what we should expect the next morning, detail by excruciating detail. Normally, the amount of detail she provided would have been overwhelming, but I knew it was important to fully understand what I needed to do to be prepared. After completing her review, we had very few questions and we were able to finally settle in for a few hours of sleep. Surgery day would be a big day, and this was our first time attending this type of big event.

I made a point to ensure each and every one I interacted with knew how much I appreciated them and their care. It was important to me to make sure the people who treat patients, everyday knew they weren't simply doing their job, they had a positive impact on me and my family. The way I view health care professionals has completely changed, and I hope that our "thank you's" meant a little something to them.

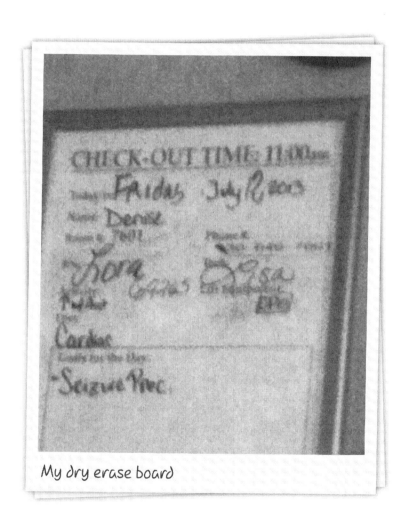

My dry erase board

GETTING THROUGH SURGERY
AND GOING HOME

MY SURGERY WAS SCHEDULED TO BEGIN AT 7:30, SO I needed to know answers to some of the most important pre-op questions. I don't know about anyone else, but I wanted to know about things like: Should I wash my hair prior to them shaving half of my head? Should I wear a bra? Would underwear be necessary? Would I be able to see my husband before they wheeled me into the operating room? How long would the entire process take?

Fortunately, the nurses and doctors answered all of our questions, plus many more. They provided us with consent forms, anesthesia forms, surgical forms, and non-directive forms. They informed us that I would be the first surgery of the day, and that I would receive my "haircut" while I was in holding between the MRI and surgery. My husband kept track of every step on **Surgery Day.**

2:00 a.m. - 2:30 a.m.	Vitals and last round of IV (Decadron)
5:10 a.m.	Starting wakeup call and last round of vitals/neuro checks
5:25 a.m.	Ativan (to help with the MRI freak out factor)
5:30 a.m.	Transport to MRI
6:40 a.m.	Transport from MRI to OR Prep Room
7:20 a.m.	Meet with Anesthesiologist (inform him that I have a very narrow esophagus and to use a small tube)
7:25 a.m.	Meet with Dr. Rabin (neurosurgeon) and do final check-up/overview
7:30 a.m.	Meet with Allie about neuro monitoring)
7:45 a.m.	Leave pre-op room with nurse and Approximately 45 minutes of prep time before surgery begins.
9:23 a.m.	Update (Incision for surgery occurred 30 minutes ago and status is – all good!)
11:45 a.m.	In recovery
11:55 a.m.	Meet with Dr. R

All great news! Tumor was slightly attached to my sinus membrane, but it was scraped closely and they burned cells a bit closer to brain.

Still non-evasive. This is good news!

Possible concerns:

- Bleeding-Which would mean I go back in for surgery
- Spinal fluid-Which would mean I go back in for surgery
- Infection-Replace dead bone with titanium plate

1:25 p.m.	Left Recovery and arrived in ICU (Room 6611)
2:50 p.m.	Spoke with Dr. S (Hospitalist) and he is very pleased with his observations. Happy with my movements
3:30 p.m.	Dr. M (Neurologist) visited and is pleased with results and neuro check. Will continue with Keppra and monitor for next couple of months
Early Dinner	Ordered chicken broth, cherry popsicle, cherry Jell-O, and lemonade
5:20 p.m.	ICU Attending Physician visited on behalf of Dr. R and confirmed good results.

Thank goodness for my detailed husband or I would have no idea what happened during one entire day of my life.

The pain I experienced, post-surgery, was like no pain I had ever felt in my life. I recall telling Dr. R I felt like someone had beaten me upside the head with a baseball bat. I'm not sure he entirely appreciated the comparison, as it may have been an insult to his handy work. But the truth was, my head hurt like hell. In fact, I thought for sure I was being punished for all of those times I stayed out too late and partied a little too hard. I would have given anything to replace this type of pain with a hangover any day. In fact, I would have traded my supremely uncomfortable hospital bed, (with deluxe seizure padding) for any night on the couch.

The light coming through the windows was too much, so my parents and husband closed every blind, turned off the TV, and closed the hospital room door. Every bit of noise and light was so excruciatingly painful. My head was wound tightly with gauze and while I couldn't see the finished product, I knew there was a lot going on underneath my mummified scalp. I needed peace and quiet.

My parents drove up to be there before and after surgery. Ron had told me how impacted they were when he called them to tell them about my brain tumor. I'm sure they must have been scared to death, and afraid of losing another child.

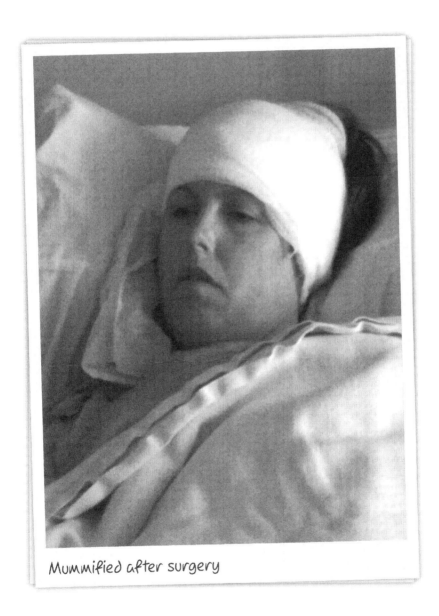

Mummified after surgery

Out of nowhere, a screaming alarm sounded. I thought, for a split second, that I was going to kill someone if they didn't get the alarm turned off. It felt like someone was blowing a gigantic horn into my ears, and my head was going to explode with pain. How in the world could a fire alarm be going off in an ICU where brain surgery patients (that would be me) were recovering?

I think my family must have wondered what in the heck was going to happen next because my speech was slurred, and I really didn't want to talk to anyone. It was almost as if I had slipped into my Missouri roots and started speaking like I was from some back woods area of the country. I knew I didn't sound like myself. I was slightly concerned, but I also knew I was just coming out of surgery and some things would take a little longer to get back to normal.

Thankfully, I had the best post-op nurse anyone could request. She had the most beautiful smile and such a terrific disposition. Every time I needed something, she was there. Everything I asked for, she got. I was, and still am, certain she is a saint. She had the brightest smile, with the straightest teeth I had ever seen. I refer to her as "Saint Nurse with a Smile." I never saw her again after that day, but she left a lasting impression I will never forget.

In addition to the nurses, my parents took great care of me while sitting bedside during my post-op recovery. It was one of those moments in life where I knew my parents both loved me so much that it hurt them to see me in so much pain. They both did everything they could to help me to the restroom, get my food trays situated, and make sure I was as comfortable as possible. For the first time in years, my parents were taking care of me like they had when I was a little girl. I was thrilled they were there, especially considering they had a farm to manage. Getting away was not always an easy thing to do, and I came to understand that was a part of owning a farm.

My husband and I made a point of making note of all of the doctors, nurses, and techs that made such a positive impact on us. The hospital has a terrific recognition program to show thanks to staff members who have made a positive impact on patients. I think we must have filled out ten to twelve thank you cards. We were so grateful for the caring staff, and appreciated what each individual did for our family. In addition to the cards, I spoke with the head of the nursing staff, and shared countless examples of the tremendous care I received. Not only did the staff treat me wonderfully, but they treated my family as if we were a part of their community of friends. We were thankful for having the experience of meeting the men and women who took care of me, as if I were one of their family. While we would not choose to go through brain surgery a second time, we would certainly choose Edward Hospital, which is not just an ordinary "community hospital."

After a couple of days in ICU, Dr. R moved me to a normal room. Ironically, it was the same room I was in prior to surgery. This was especially important because, I got to see all of the same nurses and techs I had seen prior to surgery. My head was wrapped in gauze post-surgery, and I had no idea what kind of wonderful haircut Dr. R had given me. I'm sure it would compare to a military cut, but I really wasn't worried. Fortunately, when you go through brain surgery, you put so many other things into perspective. Suddenly, your hair doesn't mean as much as you once thought. My husband was concerned how I might react when I removed the gauze. Surprisingly, there was no shock. I was more enamored with the question mark scar, sometimes called a horseshoe scar, than I was with my half-shaved head.

Each day, I showed signs of a positive recovery. I met with an occupational and physical therapist. For the first time in my life, I experienced what it was like to walk with a walker. I had never known the feeling of not being comfortable walking, or doing the everyday things, I had been doing for at least 35 years. Walking up and down stairs became something I had to take my time doing. Taking a shower required someone's help. Getting in and out of bed was something that required me to be careful.

All of these new, but old, movements and motions were intriguing. I wondered if this is what my Grandma O'Brien felt like after she had her stroke. In addition to the physical things, I worked on talking. The words didn't, and sometimes, still don't, come easily. It took me longer to think about what I wanted to say, and there were times I simply could not remember the right word to say. Things that were once second nature became new experiences.

I was released from Edward Hospital on July 12, 2013. There I was, a recovering post pregnancy, brain surgery patient, with a half shaved head and the biggest pair of sunglasses we could find. I was ready to go home, see my baby boy, and re-start my new experience, taking care of our son. I knew it wasn't going to be easy, but I was up for the challenge. I had to be careful about how much weight I lifted, how much rest I got, and most importantly, I had to give myself time to heal.

I had a few months to absorb and heal as much as possible before returning to work. I'm fairly certain my plan for going on leave of absence did not include brain surgery and recovery, on top of having a baby (via cesarean section). My co-workers and senior leadership team were extremely supportive. People who I never expected to hear from sent text messages and cards. I had a lot of thank you notes to send, and a considerable amount of phone calls to return. I was in for a full Summer.

As Ron brought me home, he came to my side of the car and helped me walk to the house. The walk from the car to the front door seemed to take forever. The sun was bright, my eyes hurt (even though I was wearing my darkest sunglasses), and I was walking with a walker that had been specially ordered for me. Who was I? I wasn't an 80-year-old geriatric patient. I was a 40-year-old active mom who just happened to have recently had brain surgery.

The moment we got in the house, I saw our cousin Mark with Zachary, and as quickly as I could, I sat on the couch and asked to hold him. The walker was parked next to the couch, and that was the last day I used it. The energy I gained by holding my son was the perfect healing treatment. I had everything I could possibly need; my bundle of joy in my arms, and my husband by my side. Nothing else in the world mattered. I was finally home (my sanctuary), and with the two people who brought me joy and happiness.

First Day Home

IT'S NOT OVER UNTIL IT'S OVER

THE WEEKS FOLLOWING MY HOSPITAL RELEASE WERE filled with follow-up doctor appointments. I had to visit my general practitioner, which I believe was just a formality. She didn't attend to me while I was in the hospital, but I guess it's better to be safe than sorry when it comes to doing what you're told. My doctor shared some great news; my iron levels were at a very good level. I no longer needed to worry about having to take iron or receive additional blood.

On July 26th, just two weeks after my hospital release, we met with the hematologist, Dr. B. We already were informed about my positive iron report, so we expected a repeat of the same from Dr. B. He started by telling us that the iron levels looked very good, and moved into the real news. The results of the pathology report (from the tumor) showed signs of Grade II cells. As a result, I would have to go through radiation treatment. I felt my eyes swell with pools of tears. Where was the good news we were expecting? Ron asked the doctor to say it all again, just so we both could understand. Apparently, the recommended radiation would help reduce the rate of recurrence. He said the chances of a recurring tumor would be much lower if I were to undergo radiation treatments. My mind immediately went to the saying, "it's not over until it's over." I should have expected something like this. Nothing in my life was ever straightforward. Just when I thought we were in the clear, and would only need to follow-up with MRI's every six months, we were thrown a doosie of a surprise.

Dr. B advised us on two radiation oncologists, and we trusted his knowledge of his colleagues' capabilities. Dr. B. knew we were a new family, and he took such great interest in my overall care while in the hospital. I recall one of the nurses telling me that Dr. B really took special interest in his patients. She said she worked with a lot of doctors, but he was very special, as she had seen him deliver news to patients and take their reactions to heart. This was the type of doctor we wanted in our corner. We knew he had a great background (because we did research on every single doctor we encountered) and he was well respected within Edward Hospital. When people go out of their way to share their personal experiences about working with a doctor, it's an important thing to remember. People can make either the worst or best comments, and based on what we experienced ourselves, we knew his recommendation of Dr. Kwon was the right one. We trusted Dr. B and when he said Dr. Kwon was one of the "best" we had nothing more to decide.

We met with Dr. Kwon a few weeks later and talked through the radiation treatment process. He advised us, I would complete 33 treatments. Dispersed throughout the consultation, was his use of the word cancer. When he asked if we had questions, we asked the general questions, like; how long will each treatment take, how will I feel, what would it feel like, etc. My last question was about his reference to cancer. At no point had Ron or I ever used the "C" word, and it was frightening to hear the doctor use it so freely when talking about me. He advised us, anytime you have cells that are abnormally affected by something, they refer to it as cancer. I felt slightly better, but still sick to my stomach. Whether benign or malignant, no one wants to think of having any type of cancer. It simply isn't a pretty word, and it brought about many different emotions. It's kind of like the word boobies. I recall my mom using the word boobies, while bra shopping as a pre-teen. It scarred me for life. Now, every time I hear the word boobies, I immediately flashback to the Jacks shopping store in Keokuk, Iowa. I was in fifth or sixth grade, and my mom informed me that I needed to start looking for bras because I was starting to get boobies. Ick! I played soccer and basketball, and every other sport in school. The last thing I wanted to consider was wearing a bra would change the way I got picked for teams when it came to playing sports.

According to Dr. Kwon, the first half of radiation might make me feel nauseous, tired, and I might start to lose some hair. The closer to the halfway point I got, I would likely experience headaches, lose more hair, and then start steroids.

I started treatments the day after Labor Day, and for the first few days, everything was uneventful. The first day was the most exciting, as I got fitted for my personalized radiation mask.

Jason Voorhees had nothing on me. My mask was much scarier, and in addition, it connected to the table. So, not only would I have to get radiation, but I would have to be connected to the table (via my new scary mask) without freaking out; because let's not forget about the fact I'm completely claustrophobic. Sounded like a hoot to me!

It wasn't until about 10-12 days in that I started to experience the side effects Dr. Kwon explained. Exactly as he had predicted, the headaches started, and my hair started falling out. By treatment #16, I had major clumps of hair falling out. I told myself I would never wear a wig, and my hair did not define me. My hair stylist said, "Your hair is just an accessory." I kept repeating that to myself each day. At no point have I ever considered myself a vain person. I have always taken pride in dressing well, and caring for myself, but vain would not be how I describe myself. At the point I started to see handfuls of hair coming out of my head, I knew I must be a little vain, or just very human, because it did bother me, and I tried to keep my emotions in check. I talked about it with Ron, and I would show him how much hair was falling out every day. I would run a comb through the little hair I had, and the look on his face revealed what he thought about the experience. The wonderful thing about my husband is I know he will always be honest with me, and when he said, "Yep, that's a lot of hair," I knew I wasn't making a mountain out of a molehill. I would have to accept it as a part of this journey, and that is exactly what I did.

At the midway point, I was put on a steroid, Decadron. It

was intended to help reduce the swelling of my brain (caused by the radiation). I'm not sure how all steroids affect people, but during this phase, I came to understand why certain professional cyclists used performance-enhancing drugs. The steroids made me feel like I was on top of the world. Prior to taking the steroids, I hadn't felt like working out in weeks.

I started slowly with my fitness routine. I first got back into my strength exercises, then moved to some wogging, (a cross between walking and jogging) and then I moved to taking longer walks. I was told I could not drive until December, so I took advantage of every moment to get out of the house and venture as far as possible. It was a magical moment, the first day I was able to ride my cyclocross bike on the prairie path. Fortunately for me, Dr. Kwon said I could ride my bike and see how I felt. He advised me not to ride on the roads, or near traffic (which we often did while training for triathlons). The wonderful thing about where we live is there are many connecting trails throughout the suburbs. I could ride for miles and miles, and simply enjoy being more than 3 miles from my house. Since I was not allowed to drive for 6 months post-surgery, riding a bike away from home was a very welcome extension of my freedom.

Happy to be back in the saddle

The first ride I took was only a short distance, but each day after, I increased the distance and rode farther from home. In the back of my mind, I remembered that I had to be careful in case something happened. I always kept my phone, some money and a Road ID strapped to my wrist or ankle. Sometimes people don't pay attention to cyclists or runners, so a Road ID was a necessity in our household. It's one of the best products on the market and has helped saved many people's lives.

At the end of September, Zachary went to daycare, and Ron went back to work. I was on my own for the first time in months, and I was a little scared. What would I do all day? How would I get to my treatments? Fortunately, my employer took care of my taxi expenses to and from radiation treatments. It was during this time I came to appreciate what I had, even more than I thought possible. My work team was incredibly supportive. I received care packages every week, and they sent gift certificates for our favorite restaurants, and even took care of some of our meals. They asked what they could possibly do to help make our lives easier, and the two things I could think of were: add a million dollars to my paycheck and help with transportation to and from treatments. Since Ron would be back at work, and I could not drive, we were left with trying to find a way to ensure I was able to get to my daily appointments without putting additional pressure on his work schedule. In addition, Ron attended Master's classes on Tuesday nights, so we had to figure out a way to get Zachary home when Ron wasn't able to pick us up those nights. My employer picked up the cost of the transportation, which was well beyond anything I could have imagined them doing. It wasn't about the cost associated with the rides. I was overwhelmed that my senior leaders would care enough to want to do something so simple that would make my family's life so much easier. It meant a great deal to us. I had a new appreciation for corporate America, and especially for my senior leadership team. They gave me an entirely different perspective on what leadership meant, and a new way to approach my job when I returned from my leave of absence.

As I continued with the treatments, I lost the majority of the hair on the top right side of my head. So, here I was with hair in the back, thin hair on the left, and no hair on the right. My solution for hair loss was a very simple one. I chose to order many different headbands and I coordinated them with my outfits. A wig would not have been my style, the so best part of the headband was being able to change them, according to what I was wearing. My first new accessory delivery was a fun one. I received three different designs and styles. Ron, Zachary, and I tried them on and immediately knew they were the right choice. Not only did Ron tell me he and Zachary would wear them to support me, but he also said he would shave his head. I could not have asked for a more supportive family. I left the haircut decision to Ron, and told him he should do what he wanted with his hair. I did not have a choice in the matter, and my hair was falling out regardless of whether I wanted it to or not. I could get it cut in a way that would lessen the impact to my ego, and that is what I did.

My Support Crew

My hair stylist, Maria, is a saint in disguise. She helped me manage my very first haircut post-surgery, and did so by coming to my home, not requiring me to go to the salon. Oh how the women in that salon would have freaked out if they would have seen my post-surgery stitches, resembling a character from the movie, "Natural Born Killers". Maria also helped by setting my expectations and explaining my haircuts would require a plan. We would start with trying to even everything out, which really meant getting the hair on the left side to cover the bald spot on the right. Somehow, she managed to give me one of the best haircuts I've ever had. The most amazing part was she made me feel like I was whole again, and she reminded me that you don't need hair to define yourself. She reminded me that hair is simply an accessory and it should complement the person I already am.

Before

After

October 17th marked the end of my 33 treatments, and Ron and I celebrated the occasion, as a couple, over a glass of wine and some tapas. We later picked up Zachary from day care and had our own celebratory evening, as a family. We had been through everything as a family, and we celebrated these moments as a family. My treatments were finally finished, and

I would begin to taper off steroids.

What I experienced during my steroid taper was beyond what I expected. The energy, I once had, quickly started to dwindle. I became accustomed to working out every day (riding my bike fifteen miles some days), and as I tapered, I began to feel less and less energetic. I hoped my hair would start to come in, but Dr. Kwon advised it would take "about two seasons" for my bald spot to fill in. Even then, I could not be guaranteed my hair would come back in the same color or texture. I guess I experienced so much change by this time, I didn't care about my hair. I didn't care if I had hair. All I really cared about was that I was going to be healthy and get to spend the rest of my days enjoying time with my family and friends.

The day after Christmas, I had a follow-up visit with Dr. Kwon to discuss the results of my post radiation MRI. I was nervous. I thought, "What if there is still a sign of the Grade II cells?" I promised myself I would not focus on the what if's and would do my best to remain narrowed in on the thought which kept Ron, Zachary, and me moving forward since June. We adopted the saying, "take it one day at a time." The saying reminded me of the 80's television program with Schneider, and made me giggle every time we said, "Just take it one day at a time." We knew there was no place in our lives for unnecessary stress.

Dr. Kwon asked me several questions about how I was feeling, what my return to work was like, if I experienced any headaches or vision issues, and he also looked at how my hair growth was progressing. At no point did he discuss the results of the MRI until I inquired about them. Surprisingly, he quickly responded with, "Oh, everything looks great. You are cancer free." He apologized if I thought there was something wrong, as he did not realize just how worried I was. The music of the four words, "You Are Cancer Free," sent me into the greatest emotional dance imaginable. I hoped for the best news, but was mentally prepared for the opposite, so it goes down in history, as one of the greatest moments of my life.

THE PATH TO HAPPINESS
IS PAVED WITH ROCKS

I HAVE SURVIVED THREE SUICIDES IN MY FAMILY, delivered a beautiful baby boy, survived brain surgery, radiation, and survived everything that comes with brain surgery recovery. The point is: I survived. My journey has not been a direct route to happy town, but my experiences have taught me that many of life's greatest lessons are learned by kicking off our comfy protective shoes and getting some cuts and bruises along the way. Some of the lessons I learned along my journey are:

- Don't ever feel sorry for yourself
- Respect your elders
- Perseverance builds character
- Believe in the power of positivity
- Whether you are religious or not, believe in something bigger and believe in yourself
- Don't be afraid to be scared.
- Remember to thank people
- Allow yourself to be taken care of

- Open your heart to others
- Hair will grow back, your heart doesn't need it to stay warm
- One step at a time, one day at a time
- Feed on the energy of others
- Make sure people know how much they mean to you
- Be good to everyone, no exceptions
- Simplify your life
- Learn to forgive (yourself and others)

I collected inspirational quotes from various sources and have saved them in my "brain tumor journey" box (which consists of quotations, card, magazine articles, etc.) One of my favorite sayings is:

You have the right to a beautiful life.

I have been extremely fortunate to have gotten the opportunity to tell my story, and I fully intend to help others do the same by advocating for brain tumor and suicide awareness. Everyone has the power to positively impact others, and that is my ultimate goal in life. Often times, all it takes is a little courage to put your story to paper, and that is exactly what I have done.

Made in the USA
Charleston, SC
15 October 2014